From Zero to $5 Million in Five Years:

A Real-Life Story with Lessons for Your Business

by
Richard Houston

Disclaimer

The information in this book is based upon my own personal opinion and experience. You should not assume any information or example in this book is necessarily relevant or applicable to your particular situation. This book is not meant to provide legal or financial advice and should not be relied on to do so. The opinions stated in this book are my personal views and are not intended as text on the legal or financial aspects of property investing, share investing or business in general, and should not be relied on as such.

While every care has been taken in the preparation of this book, the publisher will not accept any responsibility or liability for any error in the information contained in it, however caused. Readers are urged to seek appropriate independent advice from suitably qualified professionals for their individual needs.

All figures and statistics in the book are accurate at the time of publishing; however, they may be subject to change.

This book is fiction, except for the parts that are true or may come true.

TABLE OF CONTENTS

DEDICATION

Even though I wrote this book, I certainly did not do it on my own. In fact, the information in this book comes from a range of people whom I love very dearly and who allowed me to do this.

To my loving children Beck, Destiny and Stefan, I thank you and love you all so very much. Thanks for all your interruptions and attempts to capture my attention.

To my darling Dragana, I thank you and love you for so much, but in this case for the numerous coffees and chats we have to analyse the world's problems and provide solutions. Your great insights and instincts really do help me to complete my understanding of this world.

(To the reader: if you ever get a chance to have a chat with my partner Dragana, you will understand everything I have said and know how understated I have been in my praise of her here.)

Thanks to all my loving family.

The Early Years

My name is Richard Houston. I am just an average guy who has taken the time to listen, look and learn. I have made more mistakes than anyone I know in life, and yet still, amazingly, I am here today to share with you my opinions and insights.

So what are my qualifications? Basically, I completed my High School Certificate in 1979 and attempted to obtain a Commerce Degree at the prestigious Melbourne University in 1980.

I learned early in my first economics class that I was not into this stuff and that there must be something more enjoyable to do with my time.

So I quit university and started my own business. I saw an advertisement in the "business for sale" column of the daily paper for a vending machine business. I went to see a man who said he had six vending machines located in local football clubs, and that they were making good money.

It sounded pretty good to a young man who wanted to make money, so I said I was in. He arranged a loan for $25,000, and thus I started my first business. To this day I still don't know how a young unemployed university student could get a loan for $25,000 from a major bank.

Well, the money came flowing in and within 12 months I had paid back the loan...and then *smack,* my first lesson in business.

The government changed its rules and outlawed poker machines, and the business became worthless overnight.

Not to be deterred, I went off and got a job. I know, how pathetic of me, but hey, I was *just above broke* (JOB) and needed the money. So I did the right thing. I worked hard and saved money. I raised enough cash to buy my new business, a cigarette vending machine run.

I was confident that this time the government could not stop me. So off I went and bought the first five machines. In less than a year, I had some 20 machines stationed in local sporting clubs around my city.

Then it happened. The government stepped in again. It did not close me down, but they raised the prices to a point where the price of a pack of cigarettes was over $2.00 and my old machines could not handle so many coins. I had the choice of closing down again or spend thousands for the new machines that could handle the coins and notes.

The lesson I learned here was that technology can close you down as quickly as the government can.

By now, my decision to quit university was not looking so good. But still not to be deterred, off I went and began a career in finance. I started work for AVCO Finance (later bought out by GE Finance) and worked hard for two years until I became an assistant manager.

Along with the income from AVCO, my work at a second job at the cinema, and the money I received from playing football, I saved enough money to buy my first property and started living in it.

Now came my big move into banking. In 1987, just before the stock market crash, I started work with a major trading bank in Australia. I was fairly successful in my banking career, but I knew there was more.

Finally, in 1995, I left the bank with money in hand from my hard-earned savings and invested in a building technology, which my partner and I took to Asia.

Let's just say that the next four years was a nightmare. I went from owning a modest home and having a good income to nearly bankrupt.

We had spent all our money on getting a contract signed and sealed for 10,000 homes to be built in the Maldives, using our building technology, only to have the contract annulled by a certain Malaysian politician (who I think actually stole the deal).

Don't get me wrong—I am not blaming anyone for my mistakes. I take full responsibility for anything I do in life. But I did learn that doing business overseas is very dangerous, and there are lots of sharks out there who will eat you up and spit you out.

So it was with my tail between my legs that I went back to live with mum and dad. It was so embarrassing living at home with them when the debt collectors came knocking. To this day I feel sorry for my parents.

While I was overseas I did have one piece of good luck. Citibank rang me to say they would pay me $400 if I referred a person who subsequently obtained a loan from them. This gave me an idea. I did my research and saw that banks would soon start selling loans via third party salespeople like mortgage brokers.

I had no money and still owed my creditors over $100,000. Hardly the right start for any business, but I had a great idea and wanted to get it done. I was lucky enough to find a local investor who provided $50,000 in capital to build the software that would revolutionise the mortgage brokerage industry.

Over the next five years I went from nothing to generating over $1 million in profit and a business worth over $5 million.

My debts were paid off in full and my business was on fire. Then came the insight part. Someone I don't even know to this day sent me a video in the mail. Based upon the video, I started investigating what was happening in the financial world, and by 2005 I knew I had to sell my business. I did, and then three years later the 2008 Global Financial Crisis hit. My business was already sold. Good luck or good planning? I will leave that to you to decide.

The lesson here is that I have immersed myself in information and refuse to take advice from the mainstream media or the so-called experts. If I could see the GFC coming, why did experts not see it also?

That is why I am writing this book. The property market is just part of a giant worldwide Ponzi scam that will eat up and spit out anyone who does not wake up and start getting a real education.

And it was with this concept that my wife and I started Money Wars TV in 2010 to help people just like you get a real financial education, so that you can survive the coming financial Armageddon.

If you have picked up this book, then you have already distinguished yourself from the other 95% of people who just don't know where to start. So congratulations—you have come a long way already.

The top 5% of people in the world have actually devoted time and energy to designing their lives, and books like this are a crucial way of starting your journey.

Everyone has personal ideas about success and what it means. Some people dream of being millionaires or having enough money to retire in the style they wish. Others simply want to provide for their families while still having time to really enjoy life and devote time to loved ones or causes they care about.

Financial success is sometimes looked down upon by people who say it is based only on greed and ego.

I argue the opposite: that in fact you must survive, and the best way to survive (and thrive) is to succeed financially first, and then apply that success to other parts of your life that mean the most to you.

Personally, I just wanted to generate enough passive income (I will go into this later in the book) to allow me the freedom to spend time on what I felt was important in life, be it spending time with my partner and my kids, or just travelling somewhere whenever I desired to.

I know a lot of people—some rich, some poor—and they *all* have issues that arise with their partners, family, friends or work environments. Everyone has issues in life. There is only thing that distinguishes the rich from the poor. Rich people can spend money on solving their problems. And they can also afford an "escape" at times to go enjoy life despite the problems (not that I advocate avoiding your problems, but a break can be healthy and provide perspective!)

Whether you like it or not, it is better to be unhappy with money than unhappy and poor.

At any rate, well done on reading this book, and I hope you enjoy your journey. It would be my honor to inspire you to take the next step on the road to success and happiness, for you and your family.

Take a moment and check out www.moneywarstv.com and the must-see documentary **Money Wars**.

Enough about me. Please sit down, get comfortable and enjoy reading this challenging and provocative book.

I get a real high out of helping people who want to be helped, so if you are one of those people, or if you have any questions or comments, please feel free to email me at richard@fintrack.com.au.

chapter 1

Get A Dream

....

If you have no dreams or desires in life, you probably live a pretty ordinary life. I hear people say that they don't want or need to make much money, or they "just want to enjoy life every day." Well, these same people often come back and complain that they don't make enough money, or that their expenses are too high.

You see, if you really look at it closely, it is not the *money itself* people are after. It is the *freedom*. It is feeling FREE and being able to do what you want with your money and your life.

If most people actually felt the power of what money could do, they would soon jump on the bandwagon and try everything they could to join the ranks of the wealthy.

Even more important than money or power is the real command of life that you get out of being wealthy: you can pursue your passion(s) or just spend time with your kids, without the financial and emotional burdens that the poor always complain about.

I say don't settle for second best. How do you know that you cannot make plenty of money? Who said to you that you would fail, or were too dumb to make it? Were they the same people who could not make it themselves and perhaps did not want you to succeed?

As a kid in school, I was told I was ugly and stupid. Well, I would concede I may not be the most handsome man, but I reckon I have a brain and have used it once or twice.

Even when I was at my lowest of lows and everyone around me thought I was a loser, I still had the passion to "have a go." I was not going to let anyone put me in a box, especially a box labelled "loser."

I had a dream, and with a lot of effort it turned into a million-dollar business within a few years. You too must have a dream and go after it.

Don't let anyone steal your dream. You are in control. "They" (whoever they are) are not. Let others stay where they are, if they wish, while you get the best out of life.

Get inspired. Find someone or something that makes you say "Wow, if they could do that, then why can't I do something as well?"

In most cases, failure comes from not doing the thing that the Nike ad is famous for telling us to do. *Most people just don't take the first step.*

The mere fact that you are reading this book will hopefully inspire you to take the first step toward a dream.

DREAMS NEED HELP

An important part of any dream is goal setting. You must start setting small goals that will lead to big goals, and eventually then you will achieve your dream.

I found that when I was on the ropes, I would cut out pictures of families, businessmen, beautiful homes, cars and yachts, and so on. I placed these pictures on the wall in my tiny little room in my parents' basement. My dream was *not* going to die. I may have failed in business overseas, but my dream was well and truly still firing me up.

So there I was at the worst time of my life, feeling the pain of failure every day. This is where I learned the power of both PAIN and PLEASURE. The pain of failure spurred me on to fulfill my dreams, while the pleasure I knew I could get from the future *also* fuelled my desires to stand back up and try again.

You need to have some useful tools to help you stay motivated and get through the barriers that will come along—and they will come, in leaps and bounds!

Having a vision is the best way to get you out of bed and kick-start your day. I truly feel really sorry for people who have given up on their dreams and get a job just to pay the bills.

Remember the Nike ad: "Just do it!"

EMOTIONS THAT CHANGE YOUR FUTURE

Have you ever looked at yourself in the mirror and wondered, "How did I get here? What is going on in my life? Why haven't I succeeded financially today? How am I going to survive the future?"

Most people at some point in their lives will ask these questions of themselves. I think today there are even more people asking these questions as the world suffers it financial crisis.

It can be painful to take a look at your life and suddenly see that it has not panned out as you would have liked.

Have you noticed how that when you are under financial strain, you start to become very agitated and anxious? This is because your emotions start to impact your body.

At this point it is important to know that one thought, one action, or even one book can actually change your life for the better overnight. Life's journey will exposes you to all sorts of people, experiences and information. Actions and results have an impact on your financial situation. Reading this book may have a dynamic effect on your life.

EMOTIONAL TRIGGERS

When we have a emotional reaction it is often caused by what I call a "trigger." A trigger is based upon an event that cues an emotional response. Triggers can be insignificant, or they can be game changers.

You may become triggered, for example, by waiting for public transport—basically a minor irritation that causes frustration or anger.

A major trigger may well be a what I call a "game changer"—like getting a divorce, or going bankrupt. I should know—I have experienced most of these triggers (well, not the divorce one, but I have been close there too).

The trigger that catalysed my fire for business success occurred when I was at university. I was listening to some guy talk about finance and I just took it for weeks and weeks, until one day I asked myself a question. If this guy was so smart, why was he teaching an angry student like me who thought that this was a waste of time?

And it was! Now at 50 years of age, I know that the education system has been hijacked. You will not learn anything more than what you need to get a job and become "just over broke."

A J.O.B. (Just Over Broke)

As I have mentioned before, many people just go to school and then get a JOB. To me this is a real sell-out for you and your family.

Why settle for less when you don't know how far you could go?

People often think that they will be safe with a JOB, and that this is the way to go for security and stability. Then they find out the hard way that a JOB can be lost. People do get fired.

Some 26 million people in America have lost their JOBs in the past few years. Many undoubtedly thought they were safe before they were fired. It's not too hard to imagine how their lives are going now.

FEAR

Most people are fearful of something in their lives. The fear of failure or the fears of success are dominant drivers of fear in our lives. Many, many people actually sabotage themselves due to these fears.

How many people do you know who seem to get somewhere in life or work, only to implode for some reason and go back to where they started?

These people often actually have beliefs (conscious or unconscious) such as "I am not worthy" or "good things never happen to me." They may feel they don't deserve success. The deeper truth quite frequently is that they are fearful of success, and the anxiety of having to continue what they are doing or even get better.

Counteracting fear is one of the hardest things to do. When things collapse and everything around you seems all too hard, you need to hold on to something to give you the strength to carry on through the fear and to the other side of success. A vision, self-work, and life tools can give you that structure and training.

I used to wonder why I could handle so much pressure. The simple answer was not that I was Superman—far from it—but I did immerse myself in a great deal of self-motivational stuff that I must admit now has given me some backbone for facing any fear of failure.

MY EXPERIENCE

I will never forget listening to the AMWAY (yes, I know, AMWAY!) tape about a person who went to see a potential client some 2,000 miles away, and that one person enabled them to grow a business. Whether this was true or not, I did not care. It taught me that you have to go the extra mile to find opportunities for success.

I applied this philosophy to my mortgage-broking business. In the early days I drove many miles to visit potential clients. In fact, I just wanted to get in front of anyone. And then one day, it happened to me.

I had really been struggling to get my business of the ground; sales were just average. I had a lead to see a lady in a faraway town, so I went and saw her. She was a lovely old lady, but unfortunately for me she was on a pension. She wanted a loan for her grandchild and his new wife, and thought I could help. She added nothing to the deal and the grandchild was in no position to get a loan.

Now I had a choice: pack up and leave or actually take some time and discuss the options. I figured, "Well, I am here now and these people are genuinely looking for help" so off I went and spent the next two hours explaining how the system worked and what they had to do to get that new home one day.

A couple of weeks went by and then out of the blue I got a call from a man who wanted some finance. On the phone he knew his stuff and had all the information I needed. He really stacked up and was excellent to deal with. I wrote a number of loans for him, with a total worth of about $3 million, so the commission was around $18,000.

Out of curiosity, I eventually asked him how he had found me, as he had not revealed that to me earlier. It turned out he was the Old Lady's son, and she had gone on and on about how good I was and that he had to see me.

The lesson in this is that you never know where your opportunities may come from, so it pays to be always "on" and always give your all—even if you think the situation in the moment is worthless. And you have to face any fear you have and have a solid reference point when things get tough. For me, the theory from the audio tape, and this proof of the theory from my early days, will always give me the strength to move forward and find a solution.

GOAL SETTING

Okay, you probably have heard about goal setting before. How is it going for you? Have you set your goals? Have you achieved your goals? I imagine the fact that you are reading this book means either you have not achieved your goals yet, or you want to upgrade and expand your goals.

First off, you need to set your own goals, not someone else's goals or goals you think you "should" have. As an example, I had a brother who was going to university for a law degree. I thought my parents' goal would be for me to do the same thing, so I set the goal of getting into university as well.

The reality set in after a year or so that this goal was not mine and hence my motivation was questioned daily at university. In the end I quit and moved on to my real goal: financial security through business.

Once you have set your goals, you need to identify how far you will go or commit to these goals. I don't mean whether you would kill someone to achieve your goals, but what price you would pay or sacrifices you will make to achieve your goals.

I know from my experience that I have paid the price and more both financially and emotionally. Has it been worth it? YES! It has been a great journey. I would not change it. In fact, I believe that until you have had a great setback or crisis you can never truly appreciate the great times. Setbacks and sacrifices are a source of perspective.

Sport can provide a good example for this. I coached a local football team and we lost the grand final in 2008. It was really painful for me, as the team and I had invested much time, worked hard and made many sacrifices, yet we failed our goal. This seemed the end of the world from a sporting perspective.

Then in 2009 we were back in the grand final, and knew exactly what we had to do. We overcame our nerves, made fewer mistakes and focused better on our goal. The end result was winning the grand final and that day became the best in my sporting career.

So set your goals and work out what price you are willing to pay to achieve these goals.

USEFUL GUIDELINES FOR GOAL SETTING

Here are some useful tips for goal setting:

• Be honest with yourself.

• Set method of achieving your goal ("I want to own my own business").

• Set defined goal ("I want to retire financially secure").

• Set dollar goals ("I want to make $1,000,000").

• Set time goals ("I want to do it in 10 years").

Although the above is very basic, it will yield a sort of a mission statement or summary. For example, "I want to start a business that will generate over $1 million so that I can retire financially secure within the next 10 years."

You will need to incorporate a vision for how your goal may look in the future. For example, if you had the goal of a dream home, you could easily describe every detail of it at great length. You may even have pictures of what you would like to have in the home.

Good luck with your goal-setting—and remember, these goals are *your* goals.

chapter 2

The Basics of Business

....

Okay, let's get down to the nitty gritty.

You need in any good business to have the relevant structures, systems and strategies to implement, produce and deliver the product (or service) to the consumer.

Along with this, you need a risk management program to minimise any issues or problems. These can come from anywhere (and believe me, when you start becoming successful in business, your competitors will throw everything they can at you to destroy your business and protect their own income).

The fundamental foundations of any business are:

1. An idea and a dream
2. Clarity about what you want to do
3. A product (or service) that people really need or want
4. Legal protection on your product
5. Systems and procedures
6. Strong capital base to work from

7. Clear communication of roles and tasks for staff

8. Risk management

9. Strong cash flow management

Before you start on this journey to riches, you need to understand what really motivates you. I mean, why do you want to do this?

Why are you planning to build a business? Is it the money, the lifestyle, the applause? Those are great to start with, but the one thing you really need to get you through all the hard times is PASSION!

You must be truly passionate about what you want to do, and understand clearly why you want to do it.

HOW POOR PEOPLE THINK

1. Go to school

2. Get a JOB

3. Work hard

4. Save some money

5. Buy a home (their biggest investment)

6. Struggle to pay the bills until the house is paid off

7. Let someone else look after their investments

8. Retire at the same level (or less) as when they were working

9. Rely on government to look after them if they mess up

10. Live happily ever after

This type of thinking will only get you what you deserve: absolutely nothing. No risk, no gain. There is no security in a JOB, and your home is not really an asset, as it costs you money and does not always go up in value. (In fact, if you have not read my book *The Great Property Ponzi Scam*, then please visit www.moneywarstv.com or Amazon.com and check it out.)

Poor people usually assume and are resigned to the thought that they will never be rich, and some say they are not interested in money. This is rarely true. There may be some people out there who are truly fine with not having much money, but more often than not they are the ones who get support from their parents or the government welfare system. Most grown adults who are supporting themselves do find that they need and want to have enough money to live well (whatever your definition of that is).

UNDERSTANDING WHO YOU HAVE TO BE

To build a million-dollar business, you need to become an *entrepreneur*.

I define an entrepreneur as a person who possesses the following traits:

1. Balls

2. Self-motivation

3. Commitment

4. Persistence

5. Ability to evolve

6. Ability to learn quickly

7 Adaptable

8. Problem-solver

Besides having these traits, you also need to know how you will position yourself in business. I see this positioning as being one of two types.

Which type are you?

"PRICE TAKER"

The price taker deals in easily available products that are determined by you and your competitor's prices. These businesspeople rely on efficiencies from their business operations to make great profits. The price taker has a shorter path to success, but may never hit the big time as they can generate large activity for very little return. This makes them vulnerable to competitor discounting which can dramatically affect the bottom line.

"PRICE MAKER"

Price makers focus on their own businesses, not those of their competitors. They need to be able to make a product that is so much better in the eyes of their customers that they can charge more for it and command that price. In other words, they (not their competitors) define the product's worth and price. The resulting higher margins can rapidly build a profitable business in no time. The downside: you may leave yourself open to a competitor doing the same thing at a lower price.

Once you know which type you are and your business will reflect, the business plan can incorporate the strategic planning required for each of these types of businesses. I myself have had businesses of both of these types.

CASE STUDY:
MY BUSINESS

I was a price taker in my mortgage broking business. I competed by offering a better price, rather than trying to set a higher price for the superior service I offered.

My competitors charged higher prices based on a superior service model—the price maker way.

The only aspect of my business that might have led me to become a price maker was the unique software that I developed, but even with that I was not eager to become a price maker. In this business, I wanted the path of least resistance.

S.W.O.T ANALYSIS

Before you go off and build your business, it may be wise to conduct a Strengths, Weaknesses, Opportunity and Threats (S.W.O.T) analysis. This is fundamental to any real business analysis, and in most cases you may need an independent third party to give you an unbiased opinion.

If you are going to raise money (capital) for your business, you must include a S.W.O.T analysis in the business plan so investors are assured that you are serious.

S.W.O.T analysis will form the core of your decision making process. You need to confront what you are good at and what you are not so good at, and plan to capitalize on the strengths while compensating for weaknesses.

For instance, you may be a really great manager, but terrible at handling accounting. You need to look critically at these issues and build your systems and support to accommodate this awareness.

STRENGTHS

What can you do really well? What do you excel at? Is it sales, product development, or managing people? My strengths, for example, were vision and problem solving.

WEAKNESSES

What are you bad at? In my businesses, I had to face that I could not manage people well. I hated the fact that I had to motivate staff, even though I was paying them. Yet, though I might not like doing it, staff *do* need support and motivation. Therefore, if I wanted to have successful staff, I needed to put in place a way for them to get what they needed—and not from me.

OPPORTUNITIES

What are the opportunities that you can take advantage of? Is there some angle, leverage or vantage point that will allow you to sell more product or provide more services? For example, Steve Jobs created a cellular telephone that had access to the Internet, with images and video.

THREATS

What are the major threats to your business likely to be? Can someone else copy your idea? Can they undercut your pricing? These threats could even include "what happens if interest rates go up?" Threats can come from the marketplace, the economy, or even within your own organization.

GET A FINANCIAL EDUCATION

By now you should be getting the idea that you need a real financial education. And I mean the right financial education— not the mainstream garbage that will get you into trouble.

In the normal course of life, most of us don't get the financial education we really need to become effective businesspeople. You go to school and get taught essentially how to become an employee, not how to own and operate a business. So you need a business financial education.

As I see it, you have four main ways in life to make your money:

1. Be an employee

2. Start a small business

3. Build a big business

4. Become an investor

Traditional education will in most cases lead you to become an employee, which for most people means not reaching for and fulfilling the dreams that you may have had as a child (or that you have even today as an adult).

Here, however, I am helping you begin an education that will lead to #2, #3 and #4 above. We are exploring ways that will lead you to build a business, whether small or large, and build assets that you can invest if you wish.

PRODUCTIVE AND NON-PRODUCTIVE ASSETS

Any asset that does not generate income today is non-productive, and, I would argue, bad capital. The value of such assets is illusory. And such assets can actually become liabilities.

Some would term an asset that is not generating income to be a "trapped asset," where capital has been trapped inside and is not productive.

To understand this issue, let's look at what most households do.

In accounting, there is nothing fancy about calculating insolvency; if an enterprise's debts exceed its assets, then the enterprise is insolvent. And if the enterprise has less cash coming in than it has cash going out, it is deemed to be trading while insolvent.

So how does the average household stack up? The typical household is insolvent—that is, household debts exceed household assets. By the same insolvency measurement, most households are trading insolvently.

Let's look at an example of a typical household in the USA or Australia:

ITEM	MARKET VALUE	DEBT	EQUITY
Car	$5,000	$8,000	-$3,000
Credit Card	$0	$10,000	-$10,000
Home	$200,000	$225,000	-$25,000
Student Loan	$0	$50,000	-$50,000
Total	$205,000	$293,000	-$88,000

The typical household is working to pay its debts, not generating a future. This is sometimes termed "debt serfdom," where a person is in service to the owners of the debt, usually the banks.

Now take another look at the household as an enterprise. You need to differentiate between unproductive assets (trapped capital) and productive assets (free capital).

Free capital can move in and out of productive assets to earn a return, which may generate free cash flow. So in the household example, most of the assets are unproductive and contribute nothing to future cash flow.

Let's say a household owns a house with a real-world market value in today's depressed market of $200,000, and the house carries a mortgage of $150,000. On paper, the household holds a net asset value of $50,000.

But this asset is not actually productive; it produces no income, and exposes the household to the risks of declining real estate valuations.

The asset provides the value of shelter, but if similar shelter could be rented for less than the costs of servicing the mortgage debt and the many other costs of ownership, then sinking the entire household's net worth/assets into the house is not productive.

In a practical sense, this $50,000 is inaccessible and thus trapped; housing is highly illiquid and has transaction costs of up to 10%.

In most cases, when a house is sold—"liquidated"— the sale proceeds are simply reburied into another mortgaged home. The asset is again trapped and thus not deployable capital.

The same can be said of many retirement accounts that are routinely counted as assets on household balance sheets. The assets are trapped in the account until retirement, and their deployment is often restricted to a handful of risky options (investing on Wall Street, for example).

So when starting your business, learn from the average household and start taking opposite positions from those demonstrated by these households. Resolve to only have productive assets, and generate cash flow from these assets.

Learn these mistakes from the millions of households that get it wrong, and you will get it right in business.

BUILD A BRAND

Building a trusted brand is a crucial component of establishing a business. Building a brand for a company is much like building a reputation for a person. You have to earn that good reputation by consistently doing things well and exceeding your customer's expectations. Once you've built trust and have that "WOW" factor in your brand, sales will come naturally.

Once you start building your brand, be very careful about being tempted to allow the use of your brand by another company or individual. Someone might offer you money to use you or your brand for their own purposes; if the company or individual (or the partnership with the entity) ends up badly in any way, it could harm the brand you worked so hard to create and promote.

If you do allow use of your brand, proceed with great caution; do your homework and deep research to be sure of the other firm's reputation and plans. Protect your brand and its reputation at all times, as it is key to your success.

CASE STUDY:
MY BUSINESS

I was offered a large amount of money to joint venture with another property group. They wanted to use my brand to leverage their business.

I did the math and the math looked really good. I was very tempted, but I just had a gut feeling that something might be amiss.

So I decided to wait. And while I was waiting, the news came to me that the company with which I was about to get involved was about to be investigated for false and misleading statements to their clients.

The lesson here is that if you have done the hard work to build a great brand, don't let anyone else destroy it or associate it with someone or something that could tarnish it.

chapter 3

Your Business Plan

....

DETAILED BUSINESS PLANNING

If you plan to succeed then you will, but no plan at all will be a plan for failure. Most people actually start in business with just a desire and an idea, which is very well-intended, but in most cases doomed for disaster.

Without trying to burst their bubbles, I always outline for such starry-eyed big-picture-thinkers the preparation and legwork that needs to be done. Planning lays the foundation for things to go right in every area at startup and later. It outlines solutions for problems and risky events to minimise impacts. And it is the only way to convince anyone to lend you capital. Your business plan is your blueprint for the future.

I am sympathetic to the resistance you might have to business planning. I hate doing business plans myself, as there is so much detail that has to go into them, but I do understand from an investor's or banker's point of view that this is an essential document.

Once you've conducted research into the feasibility of your new business, you're ready to write your business plan.

The business plan sets the direction for your business and keeps you on track once you're up and running. Depending on what type of business you intend to start, your business plan could include these elements:

- Executive summary - a one-page overview written after your business plan is finalised

- Introduction - explains the purpose and objectives of going into this business

- Marketing analysis - looks at the industry you are entering and how you fit in

- Marketing plan - your marketing strategy

- Operations plan - how you'll set up the business (structure, location, regulations, etc.)

- Management plan - how you'll manage your business, and employees if you have them

- Financial plan - how you'll finance your business, costing and financial projections.

Business planning is an ongoing business activity; you should regularly review and revise your business plan.

UNDERSTANDING YOUR COMPETITORS

Knowing who your competitors are, and what they are offering, is also a key component of business planning. It can help you improve your products, services and marketing. It will enable you to set your prices competitively and help you to respond to rival marketing campaigns with your own initiatives.

You can use this knowledge to create marketing strategies that take advantage of your competitors' weaknesses, and improve your own business performance. You can also assess any threats posed by both new entrants to your market and current competitors.

This knowledge will help you to be realistic about how successful you can be.

All businesses face competition. Even if you're the only restaurant in town, you must compete with cinemas, bars and other businesses where your customers could spend their money instead of with you.

With more and more goods, services and leisure options being bought or researched on the Internet, you are no longer just competing with local businesses. In fact, you could find that you are competing with businesses from other countries.

Or your competitor could be a new business offering a substitute or similar product that makes your own redundant.

Competition is not just another business that might take money away from you. It can be another product or service that's being developed, and which you ought to be selling or looking to license before somebody else takes it up.

And don't just research what's already out there. You also need to be constantly on the lookout for possible new, *potential* competition.

You can get clues to the existence of competitors from:

- local business directories

- your local Chamber of Commerce

- advertising

- press reports

- exhibitions and trade fairs

- questionnaires

- searching on the Internet for similar products or services

- information provided by customers

- flyers and marketing literature that have been sent to you (quite common if you're on a bought-in marketing list)

- searching for existing patented products that are similar to yours

- planning applications and building work in progress

Monitor the way your competitors do business. Look at:

- the products or services they provide and how they market them to customers

- the prices they charge

- how they distribute and deliver

- the devices they employ to enhance customer loyalty and what back-up service they offer

- their brand and design values

- whether they innovate business methods as well as products

- their staff numbers and the calibre of staff that they attract

- how they use information technology (IT)—for example, if they're technology-aware and offer a website and e-mail contact

- who owns the business and what sort of people they are

- their media activities—check local newspapers, radio, television and any outdoor advertising

- their online presence—check online networking sites as well as their websites

Get to know their customers

Find out as much as possible about your competitors' customers, such as:

- who they are

- what products or services they buy

- what customers see as your competitors' strengths and weaknesses

- whether there are any long-standing customers

- if they've had an influx of customers recently

Find out what they're planning to do

Try to go beyond what's happening now by investigating your competitors' business strategies. For example:

- what types of customer they're targeting

- what new products they're developing

- what financial resources they have

There are other components to a good business plan, though the above elements are those I found most key in building my business model.

There are many helpful books available on business plans, both simple and complex. Some offer templates you can follow. Find one you like and use it to make sure you've covered all the bases. Not only will investors send you packing if you're missing key information, but when you hit a snag or important phase of development down the track and don't have a plan for it, your business performance will reflect that. Invest this time now, and it will save you time and money later.

chapter 4

What Are You Selling?

Hopefully you have done some research on your product or service and its market. If not, it's time to start doing some before you begin spending money on your new business.

Who is the customer you want to target? Is it 30-something women who love shoes, or 12-year-old kids who want to play games? You need to know this market intimately and define it clearly to ensure your marketing money is not wasted down the track.

Here are a few points you need to be able to define regarding your product or service:

- What is the market opportunity that you see?

- Is this an opportunity for a price taker or price maker?

- What are the predicted trends in this market?

- Will you solve a problem or need?

- What are the demographics of your target customer?

To be successful, you need to understand the word "sell" and what it will mean for your business. Selling is easy once you have a product or service that you really believe in and that is needed and wanted by your customers.

If you can master selling, then your revenues will be strong, and that is a great start to managing cash flow in your business. Here are some vital concepts to help you create a strong foundation for sales.

DEFINE YOUR COMPETITIVE ADVANTAGE

In a nutshell, why would your potential customers buy from you and not someone else? What is it that makes your product or service unique or superior?

What is your offer or *value proposition*? A value proposition is a promise of value that a customer will experience, the customer's belief in that value, and your strategy for delivering that value to the client. A value proposition can apply to an entire organization, customer accounts, or products or services.

You must be able to clearly define your value proposition.

CASE STUDY:
MY BUSINESS

In my business, I knew I had some competitive advantages. I was a small business just starting out, with little overhead and plenty of flexibility.

I saw the opportunity to attract mortgage brokers to work in my business. Many brokers complained about the ways their firms restricted their styles of doing business, and did not feel they were getting value or services for the cost they were charged to operate.

My business was known as an aggregator. Since individual mortgage brokers could not have direct agreements with lenders, they had to use an aggregator in order to conduct business. The mortgage brokers were considered "members" of the aggregator firm.

The aggregators had direct relationships with the lenders, and the mortgage brokers worked under the aggregators to lodge the loans to the lender. Lenders paid brokers a commission—a percentage of the loan— for introducing loan clients to them. Aggregators took a cut of the broker's commission.

At the time I had my business, most aggregators charged brokers a fee of around 20% of the commission paid by the lenders. In exchange for this 20% of commission, the aggregator usually provided:

- Access to a panel of lenders
- Training on loan products
- Software for assessing loans
- Marketing material to help get new clients

Most aggregators charging 20% of the commission referred to themselves as "full service" aggregators who (supposedly) provided so much assistance that they could justify taking this large cut of the action.

By contrast, my business was offering a no-frills, lower-price model to mortgage brokers that was more flexible than that of my competitors. I myself had started in the business with an aggregator firm that took 20% of my earnings and restricted me in so many ways that I felt trapped. So, my business model was to do the opposite of this.

In my model, I offered to take only 5% from my company's members, compared with the 20% percent they normally had deducted from their commission. I also allowed them the freedom to do business as they pleased, with the ultimate guarantee that if they did not like working with me they could vote with their feet and leave at no cost.

This made it very appealing for mortgage brokers to work for my aggregation services. This meant that I not only got the best brokers, but that they were motivated by freedom and fair treatment. This became evident when they started selling more loans than they ever had before.

In addition to this, I offered my famous software program, which made the work of a mortgage broker even easier. This was a big competitive advantage that positioned me as a potential "price maker."

I knew that being greedy would not make me the instant money I craved. So in the end I simply included the software as part of the services for which the mortgage brokers paid their monthly fee.

All in all, I wanted a small slice of the market that would make me what I thought was good money. To this day I believe that taking a small percentage of a large market is the best way to make a million dollars in less than three years with only three permanent staff.

My competitive advantages were:
- I was small and flexible
- I had done my research
- I was able to develop a software program
- I was prepared to take lower margins
- I had principles and standards

My value proposition was in offering essentially the same services of the big aggregators (and more, considering my software) at a fraction of the price. I was a "Price Taker."

The result speaks for itself. I sold my company for a profit of $5 million after five years.

Your value proposition will be further enhanced by your BRAND, REPUTATION and any SYSTEMS you've developed that are regarded as unique, ground-breaking or leading the industry.

For example, another added bit of value I offered brokers was our very own training academy manual. The mortgage brokers were actively engaged in helping us to write this manual, and I offered it for free to my members.

This training academy started on the very first day a mortgage broker joined us. The manual/training helped them to not only understand the industry in which they were operating, but covered the real practical side of how to make money as a broker. It was not just a technical training program based upon theories. I specifically wanted to build a training program that was interactive and provided real-life solutions to the problems that a mortgage broker encounters in this business.

This was real support and real value for a broker at my firm. The more value I provided to my brokers, the more educated, prepared and motivated they were to provide value to the customer. When they made customers happy, I benefited.

chapter 5

Systems & Procedures

....

One of the most efficient things you can do is systemise the processes of your business. Build the business on the premise that you are not there and the business must take care of itself.

I am referring to job descriptions and clear policy and procedure regarding every process in the business. This is effectively your Policy and Procedure Manual for running the business from day to day.

Systemising your business procedures with policies and procedures allows you or your managers to train staff efficiently, so that they understand exactly what is expected of them and how they should perform their tasks. It ensures consistency in process and performance.

Established policies and procedures afford you peace of mind if you are away from the business for any reason. If this happens, the business will perform as effectively and efficiently as if you were there in person. This allows you to concentrate on building the business to even greater heights.

THE CUSTOMER MANAGEMENT SYSTEM

One of the most important ways of systemising your business is via a Customer Management System (CMS). In the past you needed to buy or develop a CMS program, but now thanks to Wordpress and Joomla, you can get one already built into your website at no extra cost. I love state-of-the-art technology!

A CMS offers a strong, standardised system to help you and your staff manage customer marketing and outreach. It's a basic need for most businesses to build a customer database (or "the list," as I call it). This is a contact list of people who might buy your product or services. A CMS program enhances "the list" and its management.

A good CMS will collect client details and then allow for target marketing to those clients. This allows you and your staff to get to know customer even better and leads to greater profit in the long term.

The most basic information you need for someone on this list will be name and email address. Depending on what you are selling, you may also need to know where potential customers live, date of birth, gender, shopping habits, and other demographics.

The more information you have, the better you can break down the list to target special promotions to particular groups, as well as track who you've reached, who you have yet to contact, and even how promotions worked. It's a basic need to store client information, but it's a real bonus to be able to retrieve and sort it at any time via search filters and parameters.

Once you have the list in the CMS, you can market to the contacts by tailoring promotions, advertising and public relations to specific demographics of people who might want or need your product. This can save you time and money in marketing, and hopefully get you better results.

The CMS should be computer-based at minimum, and in most cases web-based, as today much business is done online and people may buy online from your website.

The classic CMS will:

- Give access to any staff member

- Contain all the data about your clients

- Eliminate duplicate records

- Allow automated emails

- Improve communication between you and your clients

Anything can be used as customer data, including but not limited to documents, movies, pictures, phone numbers and anything else a client will give you access to.

Note that also in today's computerised business management toolbox, sometimes CMS can refer to **content** *management system*, which is a broader type of system that not only covers clients/customers, but many other procedural standardisations.

A content management system, as a central repository, can:

- Allow large numbers of people to contribute to and share stored data

- Control access to data, based on user roles (defining which information users or user groups can view, edit, publish, etc.)

- Aid in easy storage and retrieval of data

- Reduce repetitive duplicate input

- Improve the ease of report writing

These systems are frequently used for storing, controlling, revising, enriching, and publishing documentation. They can also offer version control by automating management of the version level of existing files as they are updated.

CASE STUDY:
MY BUSINESS

I spent a lot of time in those old days with Excel spreadsheets that were exported into the old Microsoft Access databases that we used as my Customer Management System. Today there is so much better technology available that I drool. Initially I had my CMS written by software developers in Delphi, a programming language that has been replaced by newer and more sophisticated ones.

Software, websites and CMS programs are so easy to use and really cheap, yet have so much capacity. For example, today you can use either Wordpress or Joomla to build an excellent website and CMS. My new websites are all built using Joomla because it is "open-sourced," which means many programmers can add their technology to this platform, and you do not have to pay a royalty for it as you would with, say, Microsoft platforms.

Combine these with the marketing tools available today, such as social networking and Google's suite of applications, and business becomes pretty easy to conduct. In comparison, when I began my brokerage business I had to use a fax machine to send my messages out, or take out expensive magazine ads that I could not afford. Today I can spend $25 a day for Google or Facebook advertising—or talk for FREE to my Facebook friends, or share my products via forums or blogs on the Internet.

A social media plan today is a requisite part of doing business. The good news is that social media is free or very cheap to use. The downside for some new businesspeople is that there is a learning curve involved in using social media effectively. However, it is relatively easy to learn to use, and if you feel daunted by it there are untold numbers of books, guides and consultants available to help you. This is the new marketing and you would be well advised to take advantage of it.

USING CONTRACTORS

You will also need other basic systems for your business, such as accounting functions. I used an outside contractor for many of these. Using contractors is great for many tasks. It reduces the risks that come with paying long-term employee benefits, in case things go wrong with the person. It is much easier to "let go" of a contractor than an employee. Plus, some functions are simply not full-time.

PUTTING IT ALL TOGETHER:
HOW MY SYSTEMS HELPED ME BUILD MY BUSINESS

How did I use my systems, along with the basic concepts we've explored already, to build my business so quickly?

I actually started my business with the most basic of concepts:

- A concept
- A Customer Management System
- Hard work

These three building blocks, along with my three staff, allowed me to grow from having one mortgage broker (that being me) to over 1,400 mortgage brokers logging over $250 million in loans every month.

THE CONCEPT

The concept was simple but effective; as I explained in the previous chapter, it was based on my own experience as a mortgage broker (genuinely improving the experience and value for my brokers) and my vision for success by taking a small percentage of a large market. With the value proposition of better service for a fraction of the price (the price brokers were paying to other firms of my type), my concept had firm ground under it. I was solidly positioned to attract that large market.

THE CMS SYSTEM

I set out to capture as many potential mortgage brokers as I could to solicit them to my new better model of business, which would benefit them as much as it did me. I sent them faxes and I cold-called them to discuss my new "low frills, low-cost model." Initially, I was not focused on necessarily getting them to join me right away. What I cared about was building "the list"—a list of mortgage brokers to whom I could present my value proposition.

My database of mortgage brokers categorized three main types of contacts:

1. Potential mortgage brokers not yet contacted

2. Potential mortgage brokers we had held discussions with already

3. Current mortgage brokers using our services

This allowed me to keep track of the folks I had already "converted" and with whom I worked, as well as potential members at different phases of the proposition process.

HARD WORK

Using this system and applying the simple factor of hard work to my concept, I was eventually able to draw 1,400 brokers to work with my aggregation services.

In new business, many people are not prepared to do the plain hard work of starting up. It's easy to have an idea or a concept, and most do have the brains to do the work of running the business, most which is fairly straightforward. But the difficult truth is that many people trying to build a new business become paralysed when it comes to actually making a phone call or sending a fax. This may be laziness or it may be fear. Some are scared to actually take a question or having to sell the idea or proposition.

Hard work is unavoidable at startup time. I certainly put in my share at the start of my brokerage business. I even sent off some 500 faxes to brokers on Christmas Day. To this day I am glad I did it (though also sad that I had nothing to do on Christmas day but send out faxes about my business offering! These are the compromises we make sometimes, but in the end, it worked out well for me.)

THE RESULTS

These three main building blocks started the conversations with mortgage brokers that ended with a company of 1,400 members. It began with one step, and then another and another. I sent off 100 faxes and received perhaps 10 phone calls which allowed me to discuss the brokers' needs and the possible solutions that my aggregation services offered. One by one, mortgage brokers started to understand what I was offering and how they could benefit from it. And so it was that I grew, one mortgage broker at a time.

chapter 6

Cash Flow

....

Now go and make yourself some coffee, or something stronger, that will keep you awake for this part.

Cash flow is the most important part of any business. I would say it is like blood to a human. Without strong cash flow management, I can guarantee you will have issues with your business down the track.

In the simplest terms, cash flow is the process of either putting cash into your pocket or taking cash out of your pocket. But of course, it gets more complex than that.

Let's take a look.

BE A GOOD TIME MANAGER

It is very likely that if you cannot manage your time, then you will never be able to manage your money either. Being able to manage your own business requires you to manage time efficiently, and if you don't, your business will suffer (which means, of course, that your cash flow will suffer—see the connection?)

By now you have hopefully decided what your dream is and how you are going to make this dream become your reality. Yet many people can get to this stage and then fall over.

You can get to a place in life where everything seems to be going on at once and you have no time to do anything. What with the kids, your partner, and your business, there just isn't enough time in your day to do justice to everything in your life.

Therefore, before you start managing your money, you should have mastered managing your time and in particular know how to prioritise. The lack of time is exactly the reason you need to manage it more efficiently.

Good organisational skills are essential to strong time management. Some people think this means you have to be anal and have everything in its place. Well, in some respects they are right.

You cannot work on 100 things at once and have them all sprawled over your desk. Be proactive and organise everything, then pull out the one file you really need to focus on.

The same goes for your week. Look at all the tasks you need to perform and activities you will be involved with—including family, friends, fitness, chores/errands, and recreation, as well as work) and then prioritise. Schedule carefully. Use a tracking and reminder system that works for you, be it on paper or on your phone or computer. Be sure you can see the week's tasks and priorities laid out all in one place.

Understand that especially at the beginning, a new business will often mean more hours worked in a day and in a week—usually many more than a job. This is an upfront investment you cannot avoid if you want success and you have to want it enough that this is really okay with you. Your own business is not a 9-5 proposition, especially to start with.

It amazes me sometimes when people say "It's the weekend, so I will not do any work." I have news for those people: there are people all over the world who want to become wealthy, and they put no time limit on when they work. Those are the people who will likely be the most successful–and they are your competitors.

"Working" 24/7 (or being "on") is often part of how you become successful. I certainly consider myself to be working 24/7. The interesting thing is that the more you are available 24/7, the less you actually need to be involved in your business. Let me explain this further.

The more time you spend focused on your business in the early days, the more likely it is that you will experience every little problem that anyone in your business has ever had to deal with. This allows you to learn, change, and build a thorough policy and procedure manual so that later on when you start hiring staff, and managers to manage them, suddenly you are not called so much any more.

At that point, while you are still technically available 24/7, there is rarely a need for anyone to call you except for a new opportunity. That is real wealth in my world. I don't get many people calling me anymore except when they want to discuss a possible business opportunity, and this is the really exciting part of business.

This leads to another key attribute you must cultivate: the ability to delegate. The more you can delegate menial tasks to others and stay focused on building your business, being creative, and solving bigger problems, the more success your business will have. (After all, if you wanted to just be a menial-task desk grunt, you'd get a JOB, not open a business, right?)

It is much too easy for most people to become distracted by day-to-day chores and tasks that could be easily done by someone else...and end up too busy, exhausted or unfocused to LEAD.

At one time, early on, I was a real control freak. But I worked out that it is better for me to stay out of the mundane operations in the business and work ON the business. It was a hard pill to swallow, but in the end, a very important lesson to be learned. You have to realize that your time, skill, creativity and vision is too important to your company to be wasted micro-managing every little thing.

BE CASH-FLOW SMART

One of the trickiest things to navigate in business is the fine line between getting new customers and maintaining profit margins.

A profit margin is the difference between what you charge and take in for your product or service, and what it costs you to provide that product or service. For example, if your widget costs you $10 to make when you account for cost of goods, manufacturing, labour and other factors, and you are able to sell it for $30 per unit, your profit is $20 and therefore your margin is 67%.

Business profit margins can vary dramatically from business to business. For example, a restaurant that I own makes around a 15% to 20% profit margin, yet my mortgage business had about a 40% profit margin.

In any business venture, considering all the risk you take on, you need to make at least three times the amount of return you could get on your money from a bank. So if interest rates are 5%, then you need to be making over 15% profit margin to make the risk worthwhile.

CASE STUDY:
MY BUSINESS

I owned a restaurant business in a tourist area that was smashed by the Global Financial Crisis (GFC). Our clients had been mainly overseas tourists (who ended up not coming over any more due to the high Australian dollar) and local families who came up north for the sun and theme parks.

The families had suffered already from the GFC, and they had to pay for travel, accommodations, and the theme parks for the kids—which left very little in the purse to pay for food.

So there it was in front of me: a business I had bought on the basis of earning $25 to $30 per head had now devolved into a business where I could only expect to make $15 to $20 per head. At this stage I could have just given up. Instead, I just worked smarter on the numbers.

I knew the only way to get any business at all was to go down the path of "price-taking," whereby I slashed by prices just to get "bums" in seats and maintain some turnover in order to pay the rent and salaries (never mind make me any money). My profit margins were slashed, and this can lead to a disaster for any business.

But I knew that as a "price-taker" business, I needed to gain back my margins from operational management. I did this over time, slowly, but extremely effectively.

I looked at how we did everything and found better ways to do things. I even went from table service to self-serve. I reduced the number of menu items available so I could turn over the tables faster.

Next I went after the suppliers, asking them to share the pain. From day one, I always paid things on time, so that one day I could play the card that I am a good customer and that is why the supplier should reduce their prices.

Where others were suffering and not paying, here I was paying everyone on time, and so my suppliers really did not want to lose me. Thus they offered me truly fantastic deals that enabled me to regain my old margins despite the lower sales prices.

The lesson here is that if you can work smarter, then you can operate on slimmer margins—just be very diligent, careful, and disciplined about it.

CASH FLOW MANAGEMENT

Cash flow management is critical because it is the lifeblood of your business. Reasons for this include:

- You need cash flow to pay your bills

- It improves relationships with your stakeholders

- It allows the business to take advantage of opportunities when they come along

- It's great for sales later on down the track

- It allows you to sleep at night knowing your bills are paid
- It can sometimes become a competitive advantage

So what IS cash flow management?

Basically, cash flow management involves the cash cycle of a business, which is generally as follows:

1. Production of a product
2. Stock purchases
3. Sales
4. Order fulfillment
5. Invoicing
6. Payment of invoices
7. Money in the bank

Cash cycles vary from business to business and industry to industry. In most cases it can last from 90 days to 180 days—which can be a long time to wait for money to come in to pay your bills.

CASE STUDY:
MY BUSINESS

I chose a business that had a small (short) cash flow cycle.

In my aggregation business for mortgage brokers, I received the commission from the lender on the 1st of the month and then paid the mortgage broker on the 30th of that same month.

Most businesses, however, have the opposite cash flow position—such as my restaurant business, where I had to pay my suppliers for food and the landlord for the location, all in advance, and *then* sell the food to collect my cash.

The cash cycle of my aggregation business was a key driver for success in the years to come, as it allowed me to maintain cash in the business, which in turn fuelled my growth.

BE TOUGH ON PEOPLE WHO OWE YOU MONEY

When you start a business, you are not operating a charity. You must enforce strong cash flow management, which includes setting terms of credit and eliminating slow payers.

You must sit down with people who want terms from you and clearly explain the terms under which you operate. Offer them easy payment methods and efficient invoicing, so that there is no reason not to pay you.

If you come across slow payers, remind them of that initial commitment, and make it quite clear that if they do not honour their words, then you must cease doing business with them.

If you do this, you will save you yourself a lot of hassle with people who will lie, cheat and scam their way out of not paying you. For your family's sake if nothing else, be professional about this issue and collect in a timely fashion any monies to which you are entitled.

CASH FLOW INDICATORS

You need to be able to measure cash flow so that you know you are on the right track. Here are some indicators that I found extremely helpful in building a million-dollar business. You should consult your financial advisor to assist you if you have real questions.

Current Ratio

Current Assets : Current Liabilities

Current assets include cash at bank, stock, and any other asset that can be converted to cash within the next 90 days. This should be 2:1 or better.

Quick Asset Ratio

Cash at Bank : Current Liabilities

This one is down to just how much cash you have to meet your current liabilities. This should be 1:1 or better.

Debt to Equity Ratio

Total Liabilities : Equity in business

Equity is the capital or cash you have invested in your business (not including your time) and does not include any loans. This should be 3:1 or better.

Debt Servicing Ratio

Net Operating Income : Interest paid on total debt

This ratio includes interest, charges and capital repayments. A ratio below 1 represents negative cash flow, and there you have major issues.

Cash Ratio

Savings in Bank : Total Cash flow Out

This is my favorite ratio, as it tells you how many days you have to survive if you run out of cash flow coming in from sales.

CASH FLOW AND CAPITAL GAINS

A real financial education requires a person to understand not only cash flow, but the concept of capital gains.

Most people buy shares or property on the basis that the price will always eventually go up; hence in the long run they expect to make a capital gain. The biggest losers in the 2008 Global Financial Crisis were these people, as they suddenly found out that prices do not always go up and can actually go down.

Average people invest for capital gains. I think they might as well go to the casino and make a bet at the roulette wheel. I don't believe capital gains investors are real investors. They are really just traders, or people who bet on things going up or down. They don't really work on a business or property to develop it to its full potential.

True business people or investors will invest for cash flow first and capital gains second. The true investor will be happiest to receive cash flow every day, and making a capital gain when they can will be icing on the cake. The smartest person will take advantage of tax breaks and using other people's money (OPM) as much as possible.

chapter 7

Risk Management

....

PEOPLE ARE SCARED OF RISK

On a regular basis, people tell me that they don't like taking risks, and that is why they stay in their jobs. They say they would rather play it safe than take a risk in life. I often just avoid the subject with such people, but personally I think to myself that they are taking the biggest risk of all by trying to avoid risks.

Most of us know of someone who once held a well-paid job, but is now unemployed and suffering. These people tried to avoid risk, and look where it got them!

Sometimes I think these common terms or expressions are very funny:

"Job Security" (what is so secure about your job?)

"Safe Investments" (all investments have risk)

These are contradictions in terms, and there are many of them in the myths about work and business.

In this chapter I will discuss common business risks and how to prepare for and protect against them: chiefly issues with cash flow, legal issue, employee and operational issues, and brand issues.

LACK OF CASH FLOW OR CAPITAL

Let's face it: any business will carry risk. It's the nature of the beast.

In business, the main risk you will face is lack of cash flow. Bad cash flow is the key ingredient in any failed business.

Operating cash flow can be defined simply as net cash in less net cash out.

A strong cash flow position will enable a business to survive and grow even in the bad times.

What makes the lack of cash flow even more risky in a business is what the problem can spur desperate business owners to do. It's bad enough if a business does not have enough cash flow in (like sales revenue) to meet the cash flow out (expenses such as rent, wages, etc.). The shortfall in cash flow is a problem, but it can become worse as the owners of the business struggle to fund this cash flow shortage.

In most cases, businesses use short-term cash loans at high interest rates. This high-interest debt ultimately compounds the original cash flow deficit. This is a vicious cycle, and it can destroy the business.

HOW DOES CASH FLOW BECOME A PROBLEM?

Poor cash flow management, or even errors in the initial conceptualization of your business, can cause reduced or negative cash flow.

Some of the most common reasons for cash flow problems include:

- your margins are too low
- your cash cycle is poorly planned out
- your business model is wrong in the first place

- you fail to collect your money on time

- you don't have proper accounting systems in place

- you fail to have a third party oversee your cash flow

It is best to plan your business carefully and properly to avoid these kinds of problems down the line.

FINANCING OPTIONS

When a business hits the wall and starts needing cash to fund a shortfall between the cash coming in and the cash going out, there are not a lot of options.

You could go to your family and ask them for money, but this is fraught with dangerous dynamics in family relations. You know best what kind of family you have, and situations vary widely, but many families are unable or unwilling to help, and most family members will not be too thrilled with you if you are unable to pay back the money. This can affect valuable family relations a long way down the road.

You could ask friends for money. Occasionally you may find you are a lucky person with a friend who is both able and willing to help out in this way, but it's rare. My experience with this is that when it comes to money, your friends may suddenly become Wall Street bankers and want all the security in the world and a high return. They may buy you a drink at the bar, but when it comes to big money, most friends will become different people. And again, if you want to preserve a friendship long into the future, it's best not to mix business into it.

If the money is not going to come from family or friends, where could you get the money if you need it? Most businesses obtain cash from banks.

If you are going to get money from the bank, you need substantial and specific documentation. Although business plans do provide details about you and your product or service, most banks don't care all that much about how great you or your products are—they mainly care about one thing, which is how you will pay the money back. The viability of your product or service is relevant mostly because it informs how well you will be able to profit and therefore pay back your loan.

Most banks will ask you to provide them with a business plan, but the clue to their real concern is found in the bankers' actions. Why do bankers always ask for some form of security or collateral for a loan, such as personal guarantees or property as security? The reason is simple; they are usually glad to loan the money. They know that if things go bad, they can foreclose on the loan and sell all or any assets to get their money back. If that fails, they can always get a bank bailout from the government. This is how the banking world really works.

So, how will they get their money back? That will the question they chiefly want you to answer, and you need to have the answer ready and in a way you can substantiate. Expect to be able to offer them all the answers and hope that you don't get foreclosed on.

SHORTFALL CASH FROM THE BANK

Getting money from a bank to start a new business and getting a loan to help a failing business can be two different processes, requiring different kinds of paperwork, records, plans and details.

To get bailed out for a cash flow shortfall by the bank, you need to demonstrate a solution for how you will avoid the shortfall situation again. Say you loaned a friend $100 and he could not pay you back because he could not afford to. First of all, he has a cash flow problem, and secondly, he needs a loan to get over this problem. Would you lend him *more* money if you found out he was spending more than he earned? Likely you would not, as he has not shown you an ability to pay you back or avoid this circumstance from occurring again in the future.

To go to the bank with a proposal for a new business, you will need a detailed business plan explaining how your new venture will make the money to not only pay the lender back, but also make a profit in the future.

I personally think the business plan is more relevant to you as the business owner, because you need to know what the impact will be if you cannot pay back your loan. In fact, you should be able to determine what rate of interest your business can afford. You may be offered a high-interest loan, which you are so desperate to take that you fail to realise you could end up losing all your business to the lender.

NEED CASH FLOW? TRY FACTORING

If you do get into an unfortunate bind with cash flow, there is a way to keep up with your bills and expenses without exorbitant high-interest loans. It's call factoring.

How does factoring work? A business in trouble with cash flow sells all or part of its unpaid invoices, on an ongoing basis, usually 12 months or more.

A factoring company will pay you around 80% of the value of your invoices in advance (the rest is paid to you later, less the factoring company's fee) and then will collect the face value of the invoices from your clients. They also charge around 5% interest per month on the loan (you're essentially being loaned about 80 percent of your projected proceeds before they are collected) until they collect all the money from the invoices for you.

Factoring is generally only feasible for expanding a business, or for times when you don't have cash on hand to take advantage of opportunities that may come to you. It's better not to get in a position where you need it, but it beats some of the other options that will eat your business alive.

LEGAL ISSUES

There are many issues that can confront a business, but legal issues can certainly destroy you. The price of engaging a lawyer is always very high, and should be avoided at all costs.

Here are some legal issues you will need to think about and prepare for (or protect against) when starting your business:

1. Using the right business structure

How will you set up your business? Will you operate as a one-man band (sole proprietorship), a partnership, or a full-fledged corporation? Will you need a trust for protection? There are tax considerations for each type of entity. You really need to see your accountant *and* lawyer for this setup.

2. Corporate governance

Each country has different regulatory bodies, notifications and disclosure obligations, business names, and director responsibilities for companies, so you need to know what you laws you have to obey.

3. Legal Agreements

Many businesses have to regulate business and legal relations with suppliers and customers; these are dictated by the law of the land.

4. Premises
Commercial leases and property transactions are subject to rules, regulations and laws, so before you sign a long-term lease, ensure that you know what you are signing.

5. Taxation
There are legal considerations for the taxation of businesses and individuals; corporate taxation and repatriation of profits; capital gains tax; and stamp duty on transactions.

6. Workplace Relations
You must be sure to understand and be in compliance with employment law and workplace relations, as well as visa requirements for overseas staff.

7. Protecting Your Intellectual Property
This includes brand name and other trademark protection, including prosecution of trademarks as well as international and Madrid Protocol trademark applications.

8. Consumer Protection
Consumer practices law and rules govern unconscionable conduct, product liability, and mandatory industry codes of practice.

9. Resolving Commercial Disputes
The available courts, jurisdictions, regimes and procedures for resolving commercial and other disputes vary by country.

EMPLOYEE ISSUES

This is a complex topic. I could write a whole book on this one (and maybe one day I will).

There are always times when employers and employees will not agree, and there will occasionally be real abuses by both sides. What worries me most is when staff are the first to disagree or tell the business owner how to do things. It is also sad to see good people go off the rails and become negative in their JOBS and then try to take everyone else down with them.

CASE STUDY: MY BUSINESS

I owned a business in South East Queensland, Australia, and paid around $1.2 million for it. I bought the business for cash flow and it was quite good. One day, as happens in business, my manager had to leave and go on to another career, leaving my business without a manager.

My partner Dragana went and found someone whom I thought was very talented and could have risen to the task. In fact, he was probably my best manager in most instances, except for one thing. He hated confrontation, and so he allowed the staff to walk all over him. As a result, the business ceased to perform at its highest level.

I complained to Dragana about how it was her fault for choosing this guy and now the sales figures were not up to our expectations.

In her usual style, Dragana sat down with the new manager and explained that if he was unable to manage the staff in the way we required, then we would need to replace him with someone who could manage with a firmer hand.

That manager did leave, and Dragana was smart enough to have someone new up her sleeve. She hired another manager, a woman who was not at all afraid of confrontation. The coming months vindicated Dragana's decision—the numbers not only started going north, they actually exceeded even my best expectations.

The lesson here is to have confidence in yourself and run the business the way you want to. Avoid letting others run your business without some kind of investment on their part, since in business just as in life there are some people who cannot be trusted.

Just look at the scams in business from Enron and Bernie Madoff to MF Global. All these businesses were supposed to be honest solid businesses run by professional people. Obviously, reality was another story. I personally will always run my businesses the way I feel is best, and take advice from those I choose.

BRAND ISSUES

A trademark is a brand name, logo, or slogan that distinguishes your business' products or services from those of competitors. Trademarks are some of the most valuable assets of a business. The Google® brand is estimated to be worth more than $20 billion.

Regardless of how big or small the business, the value and protection of brands is critical, particularly in the online world of today, where domain names and user names can be key to connecting with customers via websites or social media (such as Facebook® and Twitter®).

To help protect your brand(s), here are four basic steps to strengthening your trademark protection:

1. Choose wisely
The more creative your brand name is, the greater the odds that it is unique. A more distinctive and create name or slogan is generally more capable of standing out from the competition and becoming a brand with real value. Which sounds like a more exciting and valuable brand—"Search.com" or "Google"?

2. Use it
The more you use your trademarks—brand names, logos and slogans—the stronger and more distinctive they become, and the more your likely customers are to remember your brand and use it to tell others about it. Using it also establishes your ownership of it should this come into legal question.

3. Distinguish it

Use ALL CAPS, bold, or italics to emphasize your brand as often as you can. Then the customer knows exactly what your brand is.

4. Apply to register it

Registration with the U.S. Patent and Trademark Office, a federal agency and part of the Department of Commerce, enhances the protection and the value of your trademark assets. Registration allows use of the ® symbol, provides substantial benefits and savings if you ever have to go to court to stop an infringement, and may help stop cyber-squatters from registering new domain names.

Plus, maybe someday someone will want to buy it or license it from you!

chapter 8

You Can Do This

....

CAN YOU DO THIS?

One man, a dog and two young employees were operating from a small 250-square-foot office making over US $100,000 per month. The average wage in those days was around US $30,000 per annum. I was making three times this much every single month.

How did I do this? Many people ask me, "how did you build a business within five years that was making more than US $1 million in profit per year, and sold for US $5 million?"

In a nutshell, I grew from being one mortgage broker under my aggregation business to a firm with over 1,400 mortgage brokers generating over $1 million in profit per year. I had recruited and motivated mortgage brokers from all over Australia to sell loan products from the lenders on my panel.

My successful strategy is detailed most in **Chapter 4**'s Case Study, but I followed all the keys outlined in this book. I had a passion and a vision; I did my basic planning; I understood my market, I knew my competition and competitive advantages; and I defined a clear value proposition. I had clear system and procedures, and I managed my cash flow wisely.

I was willing to take a small percentage of a large market, rather than try to get a large percentage from fewer customers. I made my offer appealing by offering a better fee structure than mortgage brokers were getting from other aggregators, and adding value with my special software, training academy, and a less restrictive work environment. My brokers paid less and received more by working with me, so I attracted a large market of them.

By taking 5% of that market's commissions, that was enough to generate $1 million in profit per year.

At the beginning my services were very manual—I had to do everything and there was a lot of work to be done—whereas in the end, the services I offered had become automated and the daily work was greatly reduced.

THE IDEAL BUSINESS

The ideal business, just like my mortgage broking business, needs to have a passive income or residual income component to the business. Let me give you a little financial education about types of income.

There are three main categories of income: earned income, portfolio income and passive income.

Earned Income

Earned income is income you are actively involved in generating. People who work for a living as employees or self-employed workers are generating earned income. These people generally pay the highest taxes.

Portfolio Income

Portfolio income is usually generated by buying and selling *assets* to generate capital gains—such as with buying and selling stock shares or houses.

Passive Income

Passive income does not include earnings from wages or active business participation, nor does it include income from dividends, interest or capital gains. Passive income comes in the form of doing something once—like writing and licensing a song, or creating a software program or game—and then receiving a monthly license fee or royalty for sales or usage of the product. The initial work is done once, but the income is ongoing, often for years.

This latter model is, I believe, the ideal income source and the future of business.

THE FUTURE OF BUSINESS: A MODEL

I think the future offers a great deal of opportunity for those who want to get educated and start thinking. A new model of business is emerging in which you can make some real money with very little risk.

Let's have a practical look at my new business known as **"Money Wars."** Check it out at www.moneywarstv.com. The new business is built on the foundations of past businesses, but evolves into the way business will be conducted in the future. It may be a blueprint for your business.

1. DEVELOP THE IDEA

Money Wars' mission is to provide the truth about money and a real financial education to people, so that they can become Money Warriors and win the war that is being waged for their money.

Money Wars teaches you how financial statements work and how to maximise your cash position in order to make money on opportunities.

The original idea was to educate people about money online, away from the mainstream mortgage brokerage business I was in previously.

Here are the basic components of the Money Wars offering:

Game

This is a financial education game where players learn how to better manage their money and the effects of events and actions on their cash flow.

Blog

This where we can get honest feedback from people who love or hate what we do and they can voice their opinions. This allows clients to have their ideas and concepts nurtured by Money Wars and then embedded into the Money Wars business.

News Updates

The ability to update members with news about what you are doing is an important part of this model. We do this via video emails and web seminars. E-mail newsletters (written and designed) is another way.

Software

Our Money Plan software is a practical money-management system that utilises the financial education we teach, so that Money Warriors (our clients) can use it in their day-to-day lives.

Income Opportunity

Not only will Money Wars provide financial education and money management tools and programs, we will also provide a vehicle for Money Warriors to generate passive income via our affiliate program opportunities. Why not take a look at this on www.moneywarstv.com and see what I mean.

2. USE THE WORLD WIDE WEB

Rather than be limited in where you sell by having a storefront, I wanted a business where I could reach customers from anywhere in the world, and that "storefront" is the Internet. In order to do reach customers worldwide, I needed to develop a website. I did this in a typical way, by:

1. Obtaining a domain name (in my case, "www.moneywarstv.com")

2. Obtaining a "hosting service" to host my website (this is where your website will be located virtually on the Internet, or "hosted" as they call it).

3. Setting up email accounts with my hosting service so that people can contact the business and discuss issues or ask questions.

3. BUILD THE WEBSITE

Once you have the website concept, you need to build the site. If you have some skill, you can use the templates that many web hosting services offer to their customers—some of them are quite decent. Or, if you want to outsource it and have a unique site professionally designed, you can have a design specification made and give it to a website developer who can build your website. The design specification will have all the basics of what the website would look like and what the functions will be.

As with anything in business, you want to shop around and find a truly qualified web designer and developer (the development and design are two different things; some firms handle both in-house, other times you may hire them separately). Make sure to look at portfolios and client references.

4. BUILD THE PRODUCTS AND SERVICES

For Money Wars, we developed the following interlinked products and services to empower our members:

- Weekly News Email

- Money Wars Game - FREE for Members

- Money Plan Software – FREE for 30 days, then subscription fee

- Documentary – Money Wars DVD

- Books such as *The Great Property Ponzi Scam* or *$5 Million in Five Years*

5. BUILD THE LIST

Once you have the website up and running, along with all the products and services that you want to promote, you will need to develop a membership program to build a list of people to whom you can sell products or services (such as monthly subscriptions).

This means a *Content Membership Service*, or CMS program. (Yes, this CMS is different from the CMS in **Chapter 5**, where I discuss *Customer Management Systems*. The Content Membership

Program will capture anyone who wants to join our tribe, play the game, or use our money management software. This allows us to build a list of potential people who may be interested in what we offer. Then we can email them information or offers that they may find useful.

Virtually every time you see an advertisement for Money Wars on the Internet, you will be directed to a list-building form know as the lead capture form whereby we ask the potential client to provide basic details (name, e-mail address, etc.) before obtaining access to something they want. They get the access—and we get contact information.

These days, requisite strategies to help build your list include social media outlets such as Facebook and Twitter. You can learn about social media yourself—there are many books out now that will unpack the basics for you simply and clearly—or hire a social media strategist or specialist, as this is becoming a new specialty in the field of marketing.

6. PASSIVE INCOME

Your business can generate passive income by selling a product already created (a book or eBook, game, software, etc.), by licensing a product to other companies and receiving royalties or licensing fees, and/or through subscription and membership to content or services.

The Money Wars business employs both products to sell (game, software, books) and membership. Our membership program has three levels:

1. Tribe Member – FREE membership

2. Money Warrior Member – $29 per month

3. Money Partner (Affiliate) – $49 per month

These levels allow for ongoing passive income generated from automated programs that are built once, but generate income for years to come.

FINAL THOUGHTS

The above example of the Money Wars business is the way I believe the business of the future will be conducted.

I hope you have enjoyed reading this book, and I hope I have inspired you to build your own business.

If you need some help, just email me at richard@fintrack.com.au, and I will do my best to give you my thoughts.

Once again, thank you for taking the time to read this book. Please make the most of your life and your family's.

www.ingramcontent.com/pod-product-compliance
Lightning Source LLC
Chambersburg PA
CBHW050619210326
41521CB00008B/1320